The Joy of Chemistry

A Quick Study Guide for Kids and Beginners to Learn Chemistry Using Fun Analogies and Examples

By Nervana Elkhadragy, PhD

Table of Contents

Just for you!

A Special Gift to Students

Included with your purchase of this book is our **FREE Exam Review:**
"The Most Important 120 Questions for GCSE Chemistry".

Visit the link below and let us know which email address to deliver it to.

Nervana.pro/GCSE

Introduction

Chemistry is the study of everything that makes us – and the world around us – function. It explains many of the fascinating phenomena around us. More specifically, it is the study of what everything is made of, and how the components that make up everything interact. The tiny particles that are the building blocks of everything and make up the air we breathe, the food we eat, and our own bodies, are all made up of chemicals. The study of those small particles is what chemistry is all about. It is helpful to know how particles interact to learn more about our world and ourselves and how we can live healthier, smarter, and longer lives.

You have probably heard of many types of science, including physics, astronomy, and medicine. Did you know that chemistry is a part of almost all kinds of science? Doctors, astronauts, and even chefs, need to know chemistry to do their jobs. Are you upset because your ice cream melted and dripped on your favorite jeans? Melting is a change in the state of matter, which we can learn about in chemistry. How a detergent cleans the ice cream off your pants in the washing machine is also chemistry. As these examples show, chemistry is a part of everyday life, and we experience it all the time.

It seems like a lot to learn, but there is a simple way to learn chemistry basics. It's so much fun to learn chemistry by pretending particles are people! These chemicals, the components that make everything, are just like the people you know in your own life. Like different people, the particles that make up our world have unique characteristics and different goals. They all strive to achieve those goals, but some particles achieve them fast, and some particles just don't seem to have the enthusiasm. Some are lazy, and some are active. These particles, again like people, interact and work together in an efficient way to achieve their goals. Some particles are loners and keep to themselves.

This book will teach you how the particles and chemicals that are important to chemistry act and interact. The best part is that you don't need to memorize information to understand chemistry basics.

At the end of each chapter is a "Knowledge Check" to help you see what you understood from the chapter. Remember, these are just for fun, so feel free to do them right away or after you've read the whole book.

You might be wondering, why I wrote this book. My name is Nervana Elkhadragy. I am a pharmacist by training. I earned my Doctor of Pharmacy degree from Purdue University in 2004. Upon graduation, I found myself eager to learn more and do more. My passion for knowledge and enhancing my competency led me to become a Board Certified Pharmacotherapy Specialist in 2013. Yet, I was not satisfied, I wanted even more. So, I went back to graduate school and earned my Masters and PhD degrees from Purdue University. I am now an Assistant Professor at the School of Pharmacy, University of Wyoming, and an Adjunct Professor at Purdue University. I started teaching chemistry as a side job in 2004. During my teaching endeavor, I developed strategies for turning complex concepts into simple and relatable ones. Having years of teaching experience and multiple credentials next to my name on my business card inspired me with a thought: it would be a disservice not to spread my knowledge and experiences to the world, and that was the seed thought for writing this book. I genuinely believe that young students learn best when materials are presented in a fun way. That's why I decided to write this book explaining chemistry the same way I teach it to my students. I also believe that chemistry teachers will find value in this book as they explore different ways to convey concepts. I hope students can see chemistry through a different lens and for teachers to get inspired by new teaching ideas.

Chapter 1:

How Are Particles Similar to People?

Chemistry is the study of the world's components and everything in it. More specifically, it is the study of matter. Matter is the stuff you touch and the air you breathe: it's all around us. Matter is anything that weighs some mass. Although you might argue some things don't seem to weigh anything, in reality, they do. The air you breathe is transparent, but it's made up of matter. It's just that air is a gas, which means particles are very far apart – to the point that we can wave our hands through this gas.

You probably know that not everything is gas; some things are in liquid form. You can still kind of wave your hands through the water, but it's not as easy. This is because water particles are much closer to each other than gas particles. On the other hand, solids are much harder; you couldn't wave your hands through them.

Imagine sitting in the tub taking a bath. Now wave your hands through the air. It's so easy, right? Now wave your hands through the water. It's possible, but you feel that water is resisting the movement. Now try to put your hands inside the wall next to your tub. That's impossible!

I just described the three states of matter: solid, liquid, and gas. These three states determine how "stuff" looks from the outside and the inside.

The way particles are arranged in different forms will be different. In solids, particles are tightly packed and arranged very close to each other. That's why you can't put your hands through them. In liquid, particles are close to each other, but not as tightly packed together as they are in solids. That's why you can put your hands in water or any other liquid, such as juice, soup, soda, or oil.

The three states of matter are very similar to people. I know that sounds strange, but hear me out. Some adults are always sitting on their chairs, working on a computer, or sitting in a meeting room. Maybe they're moving their hands and rolling chairs, but they're not moving much from their seats. In solids, like adults, particles stay in one spot. They don't move. They vibrate, but they're sitting in their positions and do not explore other places

Imagine you're at a barbecue. You'll notice that many adults will sit at tables, talk, eat, and laugh. They all sit next to each other, but with very little energy. Did you ever notice that the last thing many parents want to do is get up? It's hard to separate them. It's the same story with particles in a solid state. It's hard to separate particles from each other.

The second type of people are teenagers and children. They move a lot. They will spend hours in a mall walking from store to store. They don't seem to ever stop moving. In liquids, as in young teenagers and children, particles are actively moving all the time. But they don't move too far apart. They still stay together. At a party, teenagers will walk together, and they have more energy, which keeps them moving – but they're not running. This is like the liquid state: particles are close together, but they're moving. They have some energy, and it's easier for them to move further apart.

Then there's the third type. Those are the toddlers. They're all over the place! We call them "the terrible twos" because they can be a challenge. We can't keep up with the speed they move at. In gases, as in toddlers, particles are speeding; they have lots of energy and are all over the place, getting into everything unless you're careful. Little children are going to be scattered across the park at the barbecue. They have so much energy. Similarly, gas particles have a lot of energy: they're everywhere, and it's easy for particles to spread even further.

See? People and matter are similar. Imagine you, your family, and half a dozen other families went out for a barbecue. Where would each person sit? And what would they do?

Next time you go to the park, just quietly observe what people do. The next chapter will just blow your mind about how similar particles and people are! But before we move into Chapter Two, let's check your understanding of the concepts explained in Chapter One.

KNOWLEDGE CHECK:

1. In which state of matter are particles most energetic?

____

____

2. In which state of matter are particles only vibrating but not moving?

____

____

3. In which state(s) of matter can you put your hands through?Why?

____

____

ANSWERS TO KNOWLEDGE CHECK:

1. Gas particles have the most energy, and as a result, they move very fast in all directions.

2. In solid state, particles only vibrate, they do not move. They don't have much energy.

3. You can put your hands though gases and liquids! You can wave hands, and nothing will stop you. You can wave them in a liquid, but you'll get a little bit of resistance. You can also do wave your hands in a gas, and there won't be any resistance. This is because liquid particles are not tightly packed, but they are still wandering around close to each other. In gas, particles are very far from each other.

Chapter 2:

Movement Behavior of Particles: They Are Just Like Us

We just discussed how particles in a solid state are packed next to each other and can't move much. They do, however, vibrate all the time because they still do have some amount of energy. Particles in a liquid or gas state, on the other hand, move all the time. Of course, in gases, particles are much faster because they're much more energetic.

Now that you know that particles move all the time, and if they're not moving (as in a solid state), they're vibrating, what do you think would help particles to move faster?

Did you guess it? That's right! It's heat.

When those particles are provided with heat, they gain all the energy they can, and they use it to move faster and faster. If they're in a solid state, particles vibrate more strongly. They're like little toddlers: after you feed them, they get more energy to move faster and play with more life, joy, and enthusiasm.

What if there were several different-sized particles? Would one move faster? You bet! It's the smaller particles that will move faster. Imagine a race with several participants, all with different weights. One guy looks thin and light, and the other looks heavy. The heavy guy will move, but he'll struggle. It's going to take him some time to arrive at the finish line. Have you gained weight before? Did you feel slower at moving? It's the same concept with particles. Heavier particles move slower.

Figure 1. Illustration to explain the concept of diffusion. Shoppers move from busy areas to less busy areas. Particles also move from areas of high concentration to areas of low concentration.

You see how particles move the same way people move? Particles also behave the same way people behave in a busy grocery store. Suppose you went to the store for grocery shopping with your parents. You're done shopping, and head for the checkout. There's a long line that looks crowded, but you just have to take your spot at the end of this line and wait. After a few minutes, another checkout opens, and the clerk invites people to form a new line. What do you think will happen? Of course, people will move from this long, crowded line to the empty one. But until what point are people going to move? They're going to continue moving from the more crowded queue to the less crowded one until both queues are pretty equal. At this point, it won't matter, and people will choose the line at random.

This is how particles behave: they move from a more crowded area to a less crowded area. Does this happen at home in our everyday lives? It does. Remember the last time you used watercolors? When you dip your brush filled with red dye into the cup of water, you'll see the water turning red at the surface. Wait a few minutes, and you'll see the red color spreading throughout the water. Eventually, all the water becomes red. What happened here? Well, the red particles at the surface of the water saw that they were crowded, and they realized there's a whole space ahead of them that is much less crowded, so they started

Figure 2. This example illustrates diffusion of a liquid through another liquid. Colored particles diffuse through the water until it is evenly distributed.

spreading out. At one point, they became evenly distributed. They will have no preference in moving from one area to another, and will just go back to moving randomly in all directions. You can try this out yourself. It's easy to observe if the substance diffusing is colored paint: you can see the color spreading through a colorless liquid, such as water.

What we've discussed is a liquid diffusing through another liquid. But as you can imagine, diffusion can also happen in gases. Have you ever attended a wedding in which colored smoke was released? What happens after the smoke is out of the container? That's right: the smoke spreads, and particles diffuse through the air looking for less crowded places. By the time the wedding is over, you won't see the colored fumes because the particles have spread all over.

Another example of the diffusion of a gas is the smell of delicious food. Why are you able to smell the yummy burgers several feet away from the fast-food restaurant? It's because the particles responsible for the smell have diffused through the air. They moved from the crowded kitchen to the surrounding air. Similarly, perfume spreads throughout a whole room because particles of the scent are dispersed from an area with a high perfume concentration to lower concentration areas.

Particles are like individuals. They think and make wise decisions. And like people, there can be different kinds. Some people have blue eyes, and some have green; similarly, particles are of different types, some are atoms, others are ions, and others are molecules.

In the next chapter, we will explore the structure of atoms. But before we go, let's see how well you absorbed the new information in Chapter Two.

KNOWLEDGE CHECK:

1. Water particles move all the time. You put a cup of water in the refrigerator and another cup on the kitchen counter. In which cup of water are the particles moving faster? Why?

---

2. What's the difference between particles' movement in a hot saucepan and the movement of those in a cool saucepan?

---

3. Which one is easier to smell from a distance, hot or iced coffee?

ANSWERS TO KNOWLEDGE CHECK:

1. The water in the cup placed on the kitchen counter is at room temperature – much warmer than the water in the refrigerator. Those particles in the warmer place have more energy, and thus will move faster.

2. Particles in the hot saucepan are vibrating much more vigorously; those in the cool one are vibrating like usual.

3. Diffusion occurs faster at a warmer temperature because particles have more kinetic energy, and thus move faster. That's why we all enjoy the smell of freshly brewed hot coffee.

Chapter 3:

The Atomic Structure and Its Similarity With the Solar System

Atoms are remarkably like the solar system. There's a heavy nucleus in the middle, and lighter particles orbiting this nucleus. Remember the solar system from second grade? The sun is in the middle, just like the nucleus of an atom, and the sun is heavier than all other objects. Similarly, an atom's nucleus is much heavier than the particles orbiting around it. The nucleus contains two kinds of particles mixed together. One type is called "protons", and the other is called "neutrons". In the solar system, planets are smaller, and they orbit the sun. Similarly, in atoms, electrons are tiny particles that orbit the nucleus at a very high speed.

There's one more similarity between the atom and the solar system. Like the solar system, most of the atom is space; the nucleus only takes up a tiny area of the whole atom.

We know that our solar system has eight planets orbiting the sun, and each planet has its orbit and is moving in its path. Electrons are slightly different: there can be several electrons in the same orbit. Except we don't say that they're in orbit: we say they're in "shells" when we're referring to electrons.

So how many electrons are there in each shell? And how many total electrons are there? Well, a general rule is that electrons like to orbit in the shell closest to the nucleus. If there are many electrons, some will occupy the first shell, and others will just have to move to further shells. There is a maximum of seven possible shells that we know of, which would only be occupied if there were over a hundred electrons. The number of electrons depends on the element: some have few, and some have many.

For example, hydrogen only has one electron, which naturally sits in that first shell. Well, it doesn't sit; it orbits the nucleus at high speed.

What happens if there are more electrons? Some will sit in the first shell, and if there are more electrons, others will have to settle for the second. For example, lithium has three electrons, but the first shell is tiny. The first shell can only hold two electrons, so the third electron occupies the second shell.

As you can imagine, these shells are not all equal in size. Naturally, the first shell is small because it is closest to the nucleus. That's why it can only accommodate two electrons. The second shell is a bit bigger, accommodating up to eight electrons. If there are more than eight, then it's time for the extra electrons to occupy the third shell.

Now back to the solar system. Planets are attracted to the sun by the force we call gravity. Similarly, electrons are attracted to the nucleus, but not by gravity. Instead, it's a force we call "electrostatic" force. The meaning of electrostatic is that two opposite charges are attracted to each other. The nucleus is positively charged, and electrons are negatively charged; therefore, they are attracted to each other. This is similar to how magnets attract. The north pole is strongly attracted to the south pole because they are opposite.

A critical concept of chemistry that you'll deal with as long as you study science is the charge of a particle. Some particles are neutral and some are charged – and they behave very differently. Earlier, I mentioned the three types of particles: atoms, ions, and molecules. Ions are charged particles. The other two types are neutral.

Atoms have an overall neutral charge. The reason is that the number of protons is equal to the number of electrons. Hence, the positive and the negative charges cancel each other. For example, an atom of copper has 29 protons and 29 electrons. Remember: protons are positively charged, and electrons are negatively charged, so they cancel each other. By the way, your phone has many copper strips in it, and most electric wires and strips are made of this super-important element.

So, in an atom, the number of protons is always equal to the number of electrons. If they're not equal, we don't call it an atom. We call it an ion.

When there are many atoms of the same kind hanging out together, we call them an "element". For example, copper wire is simply the element copper because it consists only of copper atoms and no other type of atoms. A cooking utensil made of aluminum is the element aluminum because there are only aluminum atoms. There are no hydrogen atoms or iron atoms or carbon atoms.

Now that you know what an element is, you are ready to learn about the periodic table. But before we go, let's think about the following questions.

KNOWLEDGE CHECK:

1. Atoms have many particles. How are these particles arranged?

____

____

2. What do we call the orbits occupied by electrons?

____

3. How are atoms like the solar system?

____

____

4. What does the nucleus of an atom contain?

____

____

5. Why is an atom neutral?

____

____

6. In your own words, describe what an element is, and give an example.

____

____

ANSWERS TO KNOWLEDGE CHECK:

1. Particles in an atom are arranged like the solar system, with a nucleus in the middle and electrons moving around the nucleus.

2. Orbits occupied by electrons are called shells.

3. Each atom has a heavy nucleus in the middle and many electrons revolving around it. There's also much empty space in the atom, similar to the solar system.

4. The nucleus contains two types of particles: protons and neutrons.

5. An atom is neutral because the number of positive protons is equal to the number of negative electrons. The opposite charges cancel each other.

6. An element is a substance consisting of only one type of atom. Examples include the element hydrogen, the element oxygen, and the element gold.

Chapter 4:

Scientists Grouped Elements Similar to How We Group Kids, a Theater, or a City

Many elements surround us at home and at school. For example, you'll find in your kitchen several items that are made of aluminum, such as aluminum foil, food containers, and saucepans. The car you ride has many parts made of the element iron. Birthday balloons are filled with the element helium. Your pencils are made from the element carbon. And if your mom is fond of jewelry, you'll find much gold and silver in your house. However, many of the items around your house are not pure elements. They're more like a mixture of several elements or several elements combined together forming compounds, in which two or more elements decide to make a deal, hold a contract, and stay together.

Scientists have discovered 118 elements, most of which are naturally occurring in our universe, but some were created in a chemical lab. If a chemist discovers an element, they get to choose its name. Imagine if you discovered a new element. Would you name it after yourself? Or would you give it a funky name? Well, that's up to you: you're the boss.

So, 118 elements. That's a large number, and chemists had to develop an intelligent way to organize them. Therefore, they arranged them in a table and called it "the periodic table". Some element names are long, so scientists decided to give each element a unique nickname. They gave them a one or two-letter nickname. In chemistry, we don't call them nicknames. We call them symbols, but they are essentially the same concept.

For example, chlorine received the symbol Cl. Magnesium's symbol is Mg. Remember that just as you write your name with the first letter upper case and keep all other letters lowercase, symbols have the same rule. The first letter is always capitalized, and if there's a second letter, it's going to be lowercase.

Some symbols are a bit harder to figure out. For example, potassium's symbol is K, and sodium's symbol is Na. Isn't that strange? Why in the world would scientists make our lives more difficult? When I was a student, I always thought that Na must be nitrogen or nickel. So, what happened here? Remember when I stated that whoever discovers the element gets to choose its name? Well, that's what happened. Humphry Davy, who discovered potassium and sodium, has given them those names (Davy H, 1807).

After Davy's discovery, a German scientist, Ludwig Wilhelm Gilbert, translated Humphry Davy's discovery, but named potassium "kalium" and sodium "natronium". That led the German people to follow Gilbert. In contrast, English and French people just called these elements potassium and sodium, as Davy named them. That worked well, and was okay until scientists decided to make the periodic table look simpler and not too busy and overwhelming by giving each element a symbol.

The Swedish chemist Jacob Berzelius oversaw the creation of those symbols, and put the periodic table together (Marshall, JL & Marshall, VR). He initially gave the symbol Po to potassium and So to sodium, which made sense. However, he later gave the symbol K for potassium, following the German name kalium, and Na for sodium, following the German name natronium. Why did he do that? Berzelius didn't want Davy to get the credit or fame.

When you become a famous scientist, please give appropriate credit to those who deserve it and be humble. Keep it about the science, not about you or your colleagues!

So how did scientists organize the periodic table? Scientists organized the elements in increasing order of their proton numbers. Therefore, the element with only one proton, which is hydrogen, took the first place. The element with two protons, which is helium, took the second place, and so on. But you cannot just arrange all 118 elements in one row – that would be very long.

Imagine if you were in charge of setting out seats in a theater. Would you just place all the chairs next to each other? No, right? You would arrange the seats in several rows. Similarly, elements were arranged in seven rows, one below the other. We don't really call them rows. We call them "Periods".

Figure 3. It is challenging to arrange 118 chairs all in one row, it's best to create several rows. Similarly, scientists arranged the 118 elements in seven rows.

Arranging elements in rows naturally creates columns – scientists called them "Groups". Chemists did a brilliant thing: when they arranged the elements in rows, they made sure that all elements in the same group had something in common. That common attribute was the number of electrons in the outermost shell. Remember how electrons are arranged in an atom? The first two electrons go to the first shell because the first shell is small and cannot take any more. Electrons then fill the second, then the third shell, and so on. The number of electrons in the last shell can range anywhere from one to a maximum of eight.

Scientists made sure that all the elements in the same group have the same number of electrons in the outermost shell. This common characteristic was an intelligent choice because elements with the same number of electrons in the outer shell behave very similarly. It's like arranging all kids who like basketball in one camp, kids who like music in another camp, and kids who enjoy reading in a third camp. This way, if you're a parent and want to find your child's camp, you know where to go. If your child plays the violin, you will find your child in the music camp. Similarly, all elements with one outermost electron are placed in the first group. Elements that have two outer electrons are placed in group 2. Those with three outer electrons are placed in group 3, and so on. And since the maximum number of outer electrons is eight, we ended up with eight groups.

Figure 4. Scientists arranged elements in groups. Elements in each group have certain similarities.

There is also another excellent way to think of the periodic table. The periodic table is not just an intelligent arrangement of all elements: it groups elements according to their characteristics. This is like a city.

In a city, you have different neighborhoods, and each neighborhood has its own style. People in each neighborhood look similar and behave similarly. In one neighborhood, people are active – they are always biking, hiking and jogging. In another neighborhood, people are less active, so they use cars for transportation. You don't see anyone walking or jogging on the sidewalk. In a third neighborhood, named the "royal neighborhood", people live in castles and never deal with ordinary people. Finally, there's this one colorful neighborhood. People are close to each other, are heavy, and are generally lazier than those in the active neighborhood. They are also charming people, and they connect people from different neighborhoods. Stay with me, I'm going to explain this analogy.

In the periodic table, you have different groups. Elements in each group have chemical and physical similarities, and behave in the same way. The chemists who made these arrangements are brilliant people. They wanted similar elements to be arranged in a way that makes it easy for us to predict chemical behavior. All group 1 elements do the same exact thing: they all react with water. So, if you see an element placed in Group I that you have never heard of, you know for sure that it reacts with water. Group 1 are those active people who are constantly cycling and moving. We call them "reactive". Other elements are generally less reactive than Group 1. Those are the people who are usually slower. Some elements do not react at all. I'm referring here to Group 8. They are royalty, and do not react with other elements.

The colorful neighborhood... what was that all about? These are the elements with no assigned group number. There are 38 elements placed between group 2 and group 3. What's up with those elements? Well, they have unique attributes. We call those elements transition metals. They didn't get a group number assigned to them because the number of electrons to be involved in a reaction is variable. However, they still follow the rule of having many things in common. They are all metals, and all metals are similar in many ways. They all conduct heat and electricity. They're shiny, and are generally solid at room temperature.

Transition metals have some unique properties in addition to the typical metallic properties. The most exciting attribute is that they form colored compounds. They also help reactions go faster. When they do that, we call them "catalysts", which is just a fancy name for connectors or speeders. That's why I think of them as the charming people, who connect people from different neighborhoods. I've also described them as "heavier", and that's because transition metals have higher densities compared to other metals.

Transition metals are a bit lazier than other elements; they are less eager to attain their goals. Wait, what? Do elements have goals? They do indeed! That's what we're going to talk about in the next chapter. But first, let's review what we've learned so far.

KNOWLEDGE CHECK:

1. How are elements arranged in the periodic table?

____

____

2. What do we call rows in the periodic table?

____

____

3. What do we call columns in the periodic table?

____

____

4. Carbon is in Group 4. How many electrons would carbon have in its outermost shell?

____

____

5. Chlorine has seven electrons in its outermost shell. In which group would you find chlorine in the periodic table?

____

____

ANSWERS TO KNOWLEDGE CHECK:

1. Elements are arranged in the periodic table according to the number of protons they have.

2. Rows in the periodic table are called periods.

3. Columns in the periodic table are called groups.

4. Carbon has four electrons in its outermost shell.

5. Chlorine is in group 7 in the periodic table.

Chapter 5:

What Is the Ultimate Goal of Each Atom?

Just like people, elements have goals. What is the goal that all atoms have?

You probably know that people usually have goals. It could be to score high on the final science exam or win the next soccer game. Adults typically plan to earn extra money or get promoted in their jobs. Similarly, elements have a vital goal to achieve. Like people, some elements are good at achieving their goals quickly, and other elements seem not to care very much.

A few elements don't even need to achieve this goal because they already have it. They are like royalty, who already have the social status, the power, and the money. So, they don't need to hustle or make any deals with regular people. These are the group 8 elements. I'll tell you why they don't have goals soon.

So, what is this essential goal? It is to have full outer shell electrons. What does that mean?

With a few exceptions, this means that each atom would like to have eight electrons in its outer shell. The eight outer shell electrons make the atom happy. In chemistry, we call it "stable" rather than happy. We know from the atomic structure that most elements have fewer than eight electrons. For example, group 1 only has one electron in the outer shell, and elements in Group 6 have six electrons in the outer shell.

For atoms to achieve this goal of eight outer electrons, they use several different strategies.

Let's start with those atoms in group 7 – those are the easiest to grasp. These atoms have seven outer electrons, and they would like to have eight, so that's an easy goal. All they need to do is gain an electron, and voila! They're now happy and stable. At this point, they're not atoms anymore. They're ions. Why? Because they're negatively charged; they now have more negatively charged electrons than positively charged protons.

Now let's think about group 6. These have six electrons in the outer shell. What should they do to achieve the goal of eight electrons? You

Figure 5. Elements have goals, just like people. Nonmetals have the goal of gaining electrons.

guessed it: they will try to gain two electrons. Similarly, atoms in group 5 will try to obtain three electrons.

A goal to gain one electron is not the same as a goal to gain three electrons. Just like with people, some dreams are harder to achieve. A goal of earning an A on an exam is not the same as earning a B. For group 7 elements, the goal is straightforward and easy to achieve because it's just one electron. It's a bit harder for group 6 because they want to gain two electrons, and of course, good luck to group 5: they need three electrons.

When the goal is challenging, you'll see that these elements do not react easily. If the goal was easy to attain, you'd find that these elements are highly reactive, sometimes even explosive. That's why some elements are more reactive than others, we will discuss this further in the next chapter.

What we've discussed so far is the goals for nonmetals (groups 5, 6 and 7 are generally nonmetals). That's what nonmetals do to achieve their goals: they gain electrons. When they do so, they become negatively charged ions. Group 7 will become a negative one ion, group 6 will be a negative two, and group 5 will be negative three.

Metals, which are generally in groups 1, 2 and 3, are a bit trickier. They don't follow the same strategy as nonmetals. Why is that? Well, as you know by now, elements in group 1 have only one electron in the outer shell – imagine if they set a goal of gaining seven electrons. That would be a monumental goal, and would take forever to attain.

Instead, they use another strategy: they donate their one outer shell electron. That's right – they ditch the outer electron (or electrons, in the case of groups 2 and 3). When metals do this, the next inner shell becomes the new outer shell. For metals, that eight-shell electron exists. It's just not the outer shell. What it needs to do is discard that outer shell with the few electrons bothering it. Metals in groups 2 and 3 follow the same strategy. They give away those two or three outer electrons, respectively, and voila! They now have a shiny polished outer shell with eight fast electrons.

Figure 6. Metals have a few outer electrons. For example, group 1 metals have one outer electron its goal is to lose that electron to attain an outer shell with eight (full) electrons.

At this point, you may be wondering about group 4. I always get this question - what would group 4 do? Well, these folks are in a challenging position. If they set a goal of gaining four electrons, that's a lot, and very hard to attain. If they set a goal of donating four electrons, that's also tough, so they neither lose nor gain electrons. They share electrons with other nonmetals. We'll dive into sharing electrons later.

We have mentioned group 8 in several areas of the book. This is the royal group. They already have the biggest desire of all elements. They already have eight outermost electrons. So why would they set a goal? They don't, and that's why they don't want to react at all. We call these elements "Noble gases". One exception you may have noticed is helium: helium has two electrons, sitting in the first shell and making it full. It's full because the first shell can only accommodate two electrons. Therefore, for helium, those two electrons are making it happy and stable.

Let's review the most important concept in chemistry – i.e. attaining the ultimate goal.

KNOWLEDGE CHECK:

1. What is the goal of most elements?

____

____

2. Why do some elements not have any goals?

____

____

3. What strategy do nonmetals use to achieve their goals?

____

____

4. When nonmetals achieve their goal, they're no longer neutral. What are they now?

____

____

5. What strategy do metals use to achieve their goals?

____

____

6. When metals achieve their goal, they're no longer neutral. What are they now?

____

KNOWLEDGE CHECK:

7. Why are elements in group 8 nonreactive?

ANSWERS TO KNOWLEDGE CHECK:

1. With few exceptions, elements want to have eight electrons in the outer shell.

2. Elements that do not have goals are the elements in group 8. They already have eight electrons in the outer shell, so they don't really need to do anything. They're happy with their structure.

3. Nonmetals gain electrons to achieve their goals.

4. When nonmetals achieve their goals, they become negatively charged ions.

5. Metals lose electrons to achieve their goals.

6. When metals achieve their goals, they become positively charged ions.

7. Elements in group 8 do not need to gain or lose any electrons. They already have eight outermost electrons.

Chapter 6:

Why Are Some Elements More Energetic (More Reactive) Than Others?

Some people are more productive and energetic than others, and they quickly achieve their goals. Elements behave similarly... but why?

All metals want to lose those electrons in the outermost shell. They're bothering them. Metals want to be stable and look more like that fancy noble gas sitting on the periodic table's right-hand side. Thus, metals would love to lose those outer electrons. But they aren't all capable of doing this quickly. Some only have one electron in the outer shell, so that's an easy kick. It's just one electron, so boom! You're out. However, if that electron is far from the nucleus, that's even easier.

When the one outer electron is far from the nucleus – for example, if it was in the fifth or sixth shell, there's little attraction between the nucleus and this outer electron, so this electron is lost in a millisecond. We call these metals "very reactive". In fact, some react explosively. But if this electron is in the second shell, then the nucleus has more power to keep this outer electron in its orbit. Therefore, this metal is much slower at reacting. So, in group 1, metal becomes more and more reactive further down the group. The more shells they have, the more reactive they become.

What about having two or three electrons in the outer shell? Losing two electrons is more challenging than losing one, and losing three is harder than losing two. That's why group 1 metals are the most reactive, followed by metals in group 2, followed by metals in group 3.

What about nonmetals? Well, let's think about it. Nonmetals would like to gain an electron. Would it be easier to attract an electron into the second shell or the fifth shell?

You got it! If the nonmetal is in group 7 and has two shells, it will need to gain an electron to add it to the second shell, which originally had seven electrons and will now become eight. The second shell is close to the nucleus, so adding this eighth electron into its orbit can happen quickly. Thus, this nonmetal is very reactive, and again, it can be very explosive.

Suppose the nonmetal in group 7 has five shells. In that case, it will need to attract an electron to join the seven electrons and be the eighth electron in that fifth shell. The fifth shell is further away from the nucleus, so the nucleus doesn't have much power to attract this eighth electron into its orbit. This makes this element much less reactive.

Let's discuss nonmetals in other groups. Nonmetals in group 6 need to attract two electrons to have a stable outer shell. That's why group 6 nonmetals are less reactive than the ones in group 7. After all, gaining two electrons is a more ambitious goal than gaining only one electron. Group 5 is even lazier because it must attract three electrons.

Now let's check your understanding.

KNOWLEDGE CHECK:

1. Rubidium is a metal in group 1; aluminum is a metal in group 3. Predict which metal would be more reactive?

---

2. Both lithium and potassium are metals in group 1. Electrons in lithium occupy two shells. However, in potassium, there are four shells. Which metal is more reactive, and why?

---

3. Chlorine is a nonmetal in group 7, and phosphorous is a nonmetal in group 5. Predict which nonmetal will be more reactive.

---

4. Both fluorine and iodine are nonmetals in group 7. Electrons in fluorine occupy two shells. However, in iodine, there are five shells. Which nonmetal is more reactive, and why?

ANSWERS TO KNOWLEDGE CHECK:

1. Rubidium is more reactive than aluminum. Rubidium will need to lose one outermost electron, which is super easy. But when aluminum reacts, it will need to lose three electrons. That's a much harder goal to attain.

2. Potassium is more reactive than lithium. Potassium will need to lose the outer electron in the fourth shell, which is an easy task because it's not super attracted by the positively charged nucleus. However, in lithium, the outermost electron is only in the second shell. Thus, it is strongly attracted to the nucleus, and it will be hard to lose that electron.

3. Chlorine is more reactive than phosphorus. Chlorine only needs to gain one electron, a simple endeavor. Phosphorous, on the other hand, needs to gain three electrons – much harder.

4. Fluorine is more reactive than iodine. Fluorine will attract an electron into the second shell, which is close to the nucleus. In iodine, the electron will be gained in the fifth shell, too far for the nucleus to easily pull this electron.

Chapter 7:

Once an Atom Attains Its Goal, Then What?

Remember when we said there are three types of particles? Atoms, ions and molecules? We've explored atoms; the second type are called ions. Ions are simply atoms that have attained their goals. They either lost or gained electrons to become stable and happy.

For example, a sodium atom has 11 protons and 11 electrons, making it neutral. However, sodium has a strong tendency to lose one electron. This electron is bothering sodium and making it unstable, so sodium loses this outer electron. See figure 6, in which a sodium atom is giving up its outer electron. When it loses an electron, it will now still have 11 protons, but only 10 electrons. There are now 11 positive particles (protons) and 10 negative particles (electrons). They don't cancel each other anymore: there's one more positive particle than there are negative particles. This makes the sodium ion positively charged. We now give it a +1 sign.

All metals behave the same way: they lose the few electrons they have in the outer shell and become positively charged ions.

What about nonmetals? Nonmetals are generally in groups 4 to 8. Of course, group 8 doesn't form ions because they're already happy and don't need to attain a full outer shell. As we've discussed before, group

4 generally does not form ions because losing or gaining four electrons requires a lot of work. So, we're left with nonmetals in groups 5, 6 and 7.

Elements in group 7 tend to gain electrons. They have seven electrons in the outer shell, so to be happy, they need to gain an electron somehow, making them negatively charged. When an element is negatively charged, we call it an ion. Having one more negatively charged particle makes the atom not neutral anymore, it becomes negative, so we give it a -1 sign. I know what you're thinking at this point: where does it get that extra electron from? Well, we're going to discuss that in the next chapter when we talk about deals.

Similar to group 7, atoms belonging to group 6 aim to gain two electrons. When they do, they become negatively charged ions, and we give them a -2 sign. Those in group 5 aim to gain three electrons, becoming -3 ions

Chemists came up with a rule. When metal atoms become metal ions, we add the word "ion". For example, when sodium loses an electron and becomes positively charged, we call it "sodium ion".

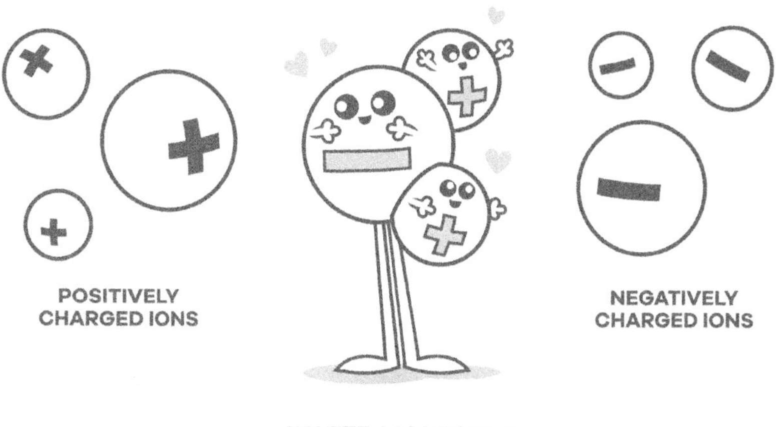

Figure 7. Water is a great solvent. This is because water is polar, i.e. it has a positively charged area and a negatively charged area. Thereby, attracting oppositely charged ions.

Nonmetals, on the other hand, are a bit different. We still add the word "ion", but the name of the element itself will be slightly changed. We remove the letter "e" at the end (if there is one), and instead add the letters "-ide." Bromine becomes bromide, oxygen becomes oxide; nitrogen becomes nitride, and so on.

Ions are very different from atoms. Because they are charged particles, they are very soluble in water. Why is that? It is because water molecules have slightly positively charged areas and other slightly negatively charged areas. Water molecules have polarity – i.e. they have a positive pole and a negative pole.

The positively charged areas in a water molecule attract negatively charged ions. The negatively charged parts in a water molecule attract positively charged ions. Because water dissolves many chemicals, it is one of the best solvents.

Many of the ions dissolved in water are common in our food, our drinks, and inside our bodies. For example, milk contains calcium ions, bananas contain potassium ions, and blood has sodium ions.

Let's check how you've advanced in chemistry so far.

KNOWLEDGE CHECK:

1. Barium is a metal in group 2. When barium achieves its goal, what will it become?

____

____

2. Sulfur is a nonmetal in group 6. When sulfur achieves its goal, what will it become?

____

____

3. Why is water a super solvent substance?

____

____

ANSWERS TO KNOWLEDGE CHECK:

1. Excellent! Barium loses the two outer electrons, and become positively charged. It will have a +2 sign. We now call it barium ion.

2. Sulfur gains two electrons and become negatively charged. It will have a -2 sign. It will now be called sulfide ion.

3. Water is a polar substance, so it has a positive pole, which attracts negative ions, and a negative pole, which attracts positive ions.

Did you figure out all the answers? Fantastic! You're doing great! Keep reading!

Chapter 8:

How Atoms Make Deals

So far, we've discussed two types of particles: atoms and ions. There's a third type, and we call them molecules. These are simply the combination of two or more atoms. This happens when two or more atoms decide that they would benefit from staying together. When they combine, they form a "bond".

This bond is like a contract that keeps two people working together on the same project for a long time – sometimes forever. In some instances, this contract is huge, and that's when they form a "double bond" or even a "triple bond". The number of bonds depends on the deal: the more significant the commitment, the greater the number of bonds.

So what exactly happens in the deal? This deal can either occur between a metal and a nonmetal, forming a compound, or it can occur between two or more nonmetals, forming a molecule.

Let's start with the type of deal between a metal and a nonmetal. Previously, we discussed that metals, such as sodium, would love to lose the electron in the outer shell because this one electron is bothering them and making them unstable. We also have established that nonmetals, such as chlorine, would love to gain an electron to complete their outer shell. What do you think happens when sodium and chlorine meet? They feel elated: they are so happy to meet each other because the sodium has finally found someone who would happily accept that outer electron that's been bothering it. And chlorine has finally found someone who would happily donate an electron to complete its outer shell. The sodium will transfer this one outer electron and give it to chlorine. Sodium becomes a happy positively charged ion, and chlorine becomes a happy negatively charged ion.

Figure 8. Ionic bonding is like a contract between two people. The metal atom donates its outermost electron, while the nonmetal accepts this electron.

This deal is called "ionic bonding" because both particles became ions upon agreeing on this deal. Sodium ions and the chloride ions will now be called "sodium chloride compound". This is simply the table salt we use on our dining table. It is a white powder, and it is very soluble in water. As we mentioned in Chapter Seven, ionic compounds dissolve easily in water because of how polar the water is.

Salt is not just one sodium ion and one chloride ion, though. There are millions of ions. After the deal is made and the contract is signed, sodium and chloride ions do not part ways. They've made a deal, so they stay together, forming a "lattice" (this is a term that describes particles arranged in millions of layers over each other). The reason they stick together is the oppositely charged ions, which are strongly attracted together. This strong attraction is why all ionic salts are solids at room temperature.

A tremendous amount of heat and energy is required to separate ions from each other and change their state from solid to liquid. The other way to separate these ions is by dissolving them in the water. In this case, the water's strong polarity will pull out each ion separately.

What if the nonmetal doesn't see any metals around? After all, metals are willing to donate electrons. But nonmetals can still make a deal with each other without metals. For example, chlorine has seven electrons in the outer shell. It needs an eighth electron to become stable. Remember that elements are not atoms in isolation: they are millions and billions of atoms. Thus, each chlorine atom is surrounded by many other chlorine atoms. All are in the same predicament of needing to gain an electron.

Imagine if you're a student of statistics, and the statistics book you need for your studies costs $200, and you can't afford it. But you know that your classmate Kyle also needs this book. So, you make a deal with Kyle: each of you will contribute $100 towards the book's cost, and you'll share it. The book will belong to both of you. You pretend it's yours, Kyle also acts like the book is his, and you're both happy. Even though no one donated a book to either you or Kyle, you still managed to make a successful deal.

Nonmetals, such as chlorine, similarly share one of the seven outer electrons among each other. Because they're both called chlorine, let's name them chlorine #1 and chlorine #2 to refer to the two atoms. Chlorine #1 will not donate an electron to chlorine #2. It will instead share an electron with chlorine #2. Chlorine #2 will also contribute one of its outer electrons and share it with chlorine #1. Just as you and Kyle each contributed equal amounts of money, chlorine #1 and chlorine #2 will share the same number of electrons.

In this case, each will donate only one electron because that's all they need: just one. Upon making this deal, each chlorine will pretend to have eight total electrons in its outer shell, making each chlorine happy and stable. That's why the two atoms stay together all the time, and we no longer call them two atoms. We call them one molecule because they've become one particle.

Many other elements also exist in pairs. We call those pairs "diatomic molecules", meaning there are two atoms in each molecule. The deal between the two atoms involves sharing a single electron from each atom. We call this deal "covalent bonding", specifically, a "single covalent bond", because it involved sharing only one pair of electrons.

Some elements won't be satisfied by sharing just a single electron pair. For example, oxygen is in group 6; it has six outer electrons, and so it needs two more to be stable. Suppose fellow oxygen atoms are only surrounded by oxygen. In that case, they have no choice but to make a deal with another oxygen atom. Each oxygen atom must contribute two of its outer electrons. One is not enough. This deal is more important, and it's a more significant commitment – two electrons from each atom will be shared. We call such an agreement a "double bond".

Similarly, because nitrogen is in group 5 and needs three more electrons in the outer shell, two nitrogen atoms make a deal together. Each atom contributes three electrons. Therefore, in this case, they form a "triple bond".

What about elements in group 4, such as carbon? Carbon has four outer electrons. Thus, it needs to share with four other nonmetals and pretend to have this nice full outer shell. It can make a deal, for example, with four other chlorine atoms, or four other bromine atoms.

Of course, group 8 won't be making any deals – they're royal!

Metals make deals with nonmetals by donating those annoying electrons in the outer shell. That is the only type of deal metals can make. We call this "ionic bonding". On the other hand, nonmetals have two options for deals. They can accept electrons from metals, and make ionic bonds, or share electrons with other nonmetals, and make covalent bonds.

Hydrogen is a unique element with a very peculiar story. Hydrogen has just one electron, and of course, this electron occupies the first shell. We know that the first shell can hold up to two electrons, and if it does, it is considered a full shell. For hydrogen, the goal is to gain another electron to join this first and only shell. Hydrogen is very special in many ways. First, it has one outer electron, but it doesn't behave like group 1 metals. Hydrogen is a nonmetal. Second, hydrogen can achieve happiness in two ways. It may opt-in to gain an electron and become a negatively charged ion, or it can lose that single electron and become a positively charged ion. Very strange, right? This is the only nonmetal that can form a positively charged ion. However, like all other nonmetals, hydrogen can make a deal with a metal, forming an ionic compound. But, much more commonly, it shares its single electron with other nonmetals to form covalent molecules.

For example, a hydrogen atom can deal with another hydrogen atom and form a hydrogen molecule. This hydrogen molecule is a dangerous one: it catches fire quickly and just isn't an easy-to-handle chemical. Hydrogen can also form a covalent bond with many other nonmetals. The options are endless. Let's explore a few of these options.

Hydrogen can make a deal with oxygen. But this one is different. Oxygen is in group 6, so it needs two more electrons. To make a deal with hydrogen, it will request the participation of two hydrogen atoms, and not just one. One atom of hydrogen will make oxygen only have seven outer electrons. That's not enough, we need two hydrogens. Thus, when hydrogen combines with oxygen, they form H2O, i.e. two hydrogen atoms, and one oxygen atom.

Similarly, hydrogen can also make a deal with nitrogen. But this time, nitrogen will demand the participation of three hydrogen atoms, because nitrogen is in Group 5, and it needs three electrons to make the magic eight. Thus, when hydrogen combines with nitrogen, they form NH3, i.e. three hydrogen atoms, and one nitrogen atom.

What about carbon? Carbon does the same kind of deal as other nonmetals. It's in group 4, so when combining with hydrogen, it will make a deal with four hydrogen atoms, forming CH4.

Making deals is like a game: the options are endless, but they're fun.

Let's check how you're doing.

KNOWLEDGE CHECK:

1. Calcium is a metal in group 2, oxygen is a nonmetal in group 6. They find each other... what do you think they'll do?

____

____

2.Bromine is a nonmetal in group 7, and there aren't any metals around. How can bromine make a deal so it achieves its goal?

____

____

3. Carbon is in group 4; chlorine is in group 7. If carbon decides to make a deal with the element chlorine, how will the contract look?

____

____

4. Nitrogen is in group 5; fluorine is in group 7. If nitrogen decides to deal with the element fluorine, how will the contract look?

____

____

ANSWERS TO KNOWLEDGE CHECK:

1. Calcium and oxygen are happy to see each other, and make a deal together. Calcium has two outer electrons, which it would love to donate. Oxygen has six outer electrons, and needs to gain two electrons. Calcium will happily transfer the two electrons to oxygen, and they'll both be happy forming an ionic compound called calcium oxide.

2. Bromine will pair up with another bromine; each of the two atoms will share one of its outer electrons, forming a single bond. That's why bromine exists in pairs called diatomic covalent molecules.

3. Carbon has four outer electrons, so it needs four other electrons. Chlorine can only share one electron because it requires one electron to complete its outer shell. Therefore, carbon will demand the participation of four chlorine atoms. They will form a covalent molecule called carbon tetrachloride.

4. Nitrogen has five outer electrons, so it needs three more. Fluorine only needs to share one, so nitrogen will demand the participation of three fluorine atoms. They will form a covalent molecule called nitrogen trifluoride.

If you had fun reading this book, please leave a 1-click review.

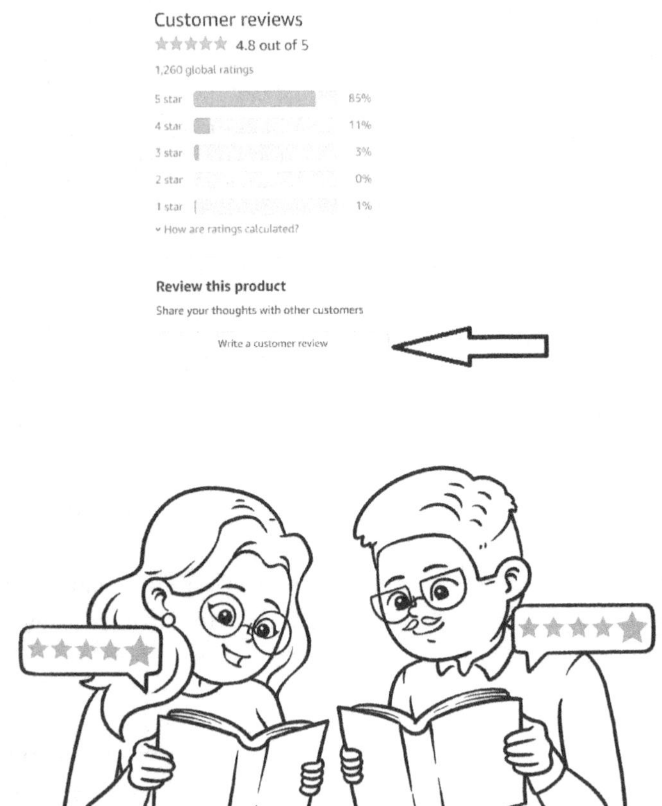

I would really appreciate it if you could just take 60 seconds to write a brief review, even if it's just a few sentences! Your opinion matters a lot!

Conclusion

See? Chemistry is fun! Don't be afraid to explore, experiment, and observe the world around you armed with this knowledge. Understanding the basics you read in this book will help you start your path into any of the sciences. Not only is chemistry the study of the building blocks of the world and everything in it, but it is also the building block of all sciences.

Now you know the basics of chemistry: the three states of matter (solid, liquid and gas), the different types of particles and how they react, move, and bond with one another, and the arrangement of elements in the periodic table. The best part is that we learned how they could relate to us and things in our everyday lives!

Now, when you see the ice melt, you'll know that it's because the heat gives particles energy, and they're moving faster, changing the form from a solid to a liquid. If you boil water, you'll know that the particles are moving faster and changing from a liquid to a gas. You also know why salts are very soluble in water. Understanding the chemical world around (and inside) us is exciting and can teach us a lot about ourselves. From now on, when you study chemistry, imagine that particles are people; they make wise decisions and deals. Now go out there and learn with fun!

Just for you!

A Special Gift to Students

Included with your purchase of this book is our FREE Exam Review: "The Most Important 120 Questions for GCSE Chemistry".

Visit the link below and let us know which email address to deliver it to.

Nervana.pro/GCSE

Resources

Davy, H. (1807). I. The Bakerian Lecture, on some chemical agencies of electricity. Philosophical Transactions of the Royal Society of London, (97), 1-56.

Gallagher, R., & Ingram, P. (2015). Complete Chemistry for Cambridge IGCSE®. Oxford University Press-Children.

Marshall, J. L., & Marshall, V. R. JOns Jacob Berzelius.

Made in United States
Orlando, FL
28 September 2024